Contents

Introduction

If you are looking for inspiration on how to plan a successful 'special day' for the children in your early years setting then this is the book for you! The Little Book of Special Days offers exciting ideas on different 'special days' that can be easily set up in an early years setting – turning an ordinary day into a special day!

How to use this book

The book is split into two sections: Themed Days and Festivals and Celebrations. Themed Days are based on a theme or topic which children will find fascinating – such as Minibeasts, Fairies or Moving House. The days in Festivals and Celebrations are based on popular cultural events which the children in your setting may or may not be familiar with and are an opportunity for children to learn about other cultures and traditions. These days include Easter, Diwali and Chinese New Year.

Whether a theme or a festival, for each special day you will find the following features:

▶ What you need

▶ What you do

▶ Ready for more?

▶ Links to the Early Learning Goals

A main activity is accompanied by a variety of complementary activities which you could set up alongside the main activity or in a follow up session. All resources suggested are easily accessible and inexpensive.

Sometimes an activity may kick start your own fabulous special day! It is easy to plan outcomes for our children but it is important to note that as Drake (2007) says, we need to "acknowledge that learning is not always confined to what has been directly planned or intended by the adult" and to reiterate this Bruce (2004) also says on the subject "investigations can take many different forms and lead to different outcomes". As practitioners, we need to value all learning, not solely the intended learning.

The Early Learning Goals

It is important to make sure that whatever special day you choose, that play is at the centre of the planning because it supports and provokes learning in all areas of development.

Play is holistic and as such this book tries to illustrate that any special day contains elements of learning from all six areas of development.

The six areas of Learning and Development:

Personal, Social and Emotional Development (PSED)

- Continue to be interested, excited and motivated to learn.
- Be confident to try new activities, initiate ideas and speak in a familiar group.
- Maintain attention, concentrate, and sit quietly when appropriate.
- Respond to significant experiences, showing a range of feelings when appropriate.
- Have a developing awareness of their own needs, views and feelings, and be sensitive to the needs, views and feelings of others.
- Have a developing respect for their own cultures and beliefs and those of other people.
- Form good relationships with adults and peers.
- Work as part of a group or class, taking turns and sharing fairly, understanding that there needs to be agreed values and codes of behaviour for groups of people, including adults and children, to work together harmoniously.
- Understand what is right, what is wrong and why.
- Consider the consequences of their words and actions for themselves and others.
- Dress and undress independently and manage their own personal hygiene.
- Select and use activities and resources independently.
- Understand that people have different needs, views, cultures and beliefs, that need to be treated with respect.
- Understand that they can expect others to treat their needs, views, cultures and beliefs with respect.

Communication, Language and Literacy (CLL)

- Interact with others, negotiating plans and activities and taking turns in conversation.
- Enjoy listening to and using spoken and written language, and readily turn to it in their play and learning.
- Sustain attentive listening, responding to what they have heard with relevant comments, questions or actions.

- Listen with enjoyment, and respond to stories, songs and other music, rhymes and poems and make up their own stories, songs, rhymes and poems.
- Extend their vocabulary, exploring the meanings and sounds of new words.
- Speak clearly and audibly with confidence and control and show awareness of the listener.
- Use language to imagine and recreate roles and experiences.
- Use talk to organise, sequence and clarify thinking, ideas, feelings and events.
- Hear and say sounds in words in the order in which they occur.
- Link sounds to letters, naming and sounding the letters of the alphabet.
- Use their phonic knowledge to write simple regular words and make phonetically plausible attempts at more complex words.
- Explore and experiment with sounds, words and texts.
- Retell narratives in the correct sequence, drawing on language patterns of stories.
- Read a range of familiar and common words and simple sentences independently.
- Know that print carries meaning and, in English, is read from left to right and top to bottom.
- Show an understanding of the elements of stories, such as main character, sequence of events and openings, and how information can be found in non-fiction texts to answer questions about where, who, why and how.
- Attempt writing for different purposes, using features of different forms such as lists, stories and instructions.
- Write their own names and other things such as labels and captions, and begin to form simple sentences, sometimes using punctuation.
- Use a pencil and hold it effectively to form recognisable letters, most of which are correctly formed.

Problem Solving, Reasoning and Numeracy (PSRN)

- Say and use number names in order in familiar contexts.
- Count reliably up to ten everyday objects.
- Recognise numerals 1 to 9.
- Use developing mathematical ideas and methods to solve practical problems.
- In practical activities and discussion, begin to use the vocabulary involved in adding and subtracting.

- Use language such as 'more' or 'less' to compare two numbers.
- Find one more or one less than a number from one to ten.
- Begin to relate addition to combining two groups of objects and subtraction to 'taking away'.
- Use language such as 'greater', 'smaller', 'heavier' or 'lighter' to compare quantities.
- Talk about, recognise and recreate simple patterns.
- Use language such as 'circle' or 'bigger' to describe the shape and size of solids and flat shapes.
- Use everyday words to describe position.

Knowledge and Understanding of the World (KUW)
- Investigate objects and materials by using all of their senses as appropriate.
- Find out about, and identify, some features of living things, objects and events they observe.
- Look closely at similarities, differences, patterns and change.
- Ask questions about why things happen and how things work.
- Build and construct with a wide range of objects, selecting appropriate resources and adapting their work where necessary.
- Select the tools and techniques they need to shape, assemble and join materials they are using.
- Find out about and identify the uses of everyday technology and use information and communication technology and programmable toys to support their learning.
- Find out about past and present events in their own lives, and in those of their families and other people they know.
- Observe, find out about and identify features in the place they live and the natural world.
- Find out about their environment, and talk about those features they like and dislike.
- Begin to know about their own cultures and beliefs and those of other people.

Physical Development (PD)
- Move with confidence, imagination and in safety.
- Move with control and coordination.
- Travel around, under, over and through balancing and climbing equipment.
- Show awareness of space, of themselves and of others.
- Recognise the importance of keeping healthy, and those things which contribute to this.
- Recognise the changes that happen to their bodies when they are active.
- Use a range of small and large equipment.
- Handle tools, objects, construction and malleable materials safely and with increasing control.

Creative Development (CD)
- Respond in a variety of ways to what they see, hear, smell, touch and feel.
- Express and communicate their ideas, thoughts and feelings by using a widening range of materials, suitable tools, imaginative and role-play, movement, designing and making, and a variety of songs and musical instruments.
- Explore colour, texture, shape, form and space in two or three dimensions.
- Recognise and explore how sounds can be changed, sing simple songs from memory, recognise repeated sounds and sound patterns and match movements to music.
- Use their imagination in art and design, music, dance, imaginative and role-play and stories.

Please note: On each activity page, links to the goals are referenced as, for example, PD 7 for Physical Development – Use a range of small and large equipment.

References

BRUCE, T (2004) Developing learning in early childhood.
Trowbridge: Cromwell Press

DEPARTMENT FOR CHILDREN, SCHOOLS AND FAMILIES (2008) The Practice Guidance for the Early Years Foundation Stage
Nottingham: DCSF

DRAKE J, (2005) Planning Children's Play and Learning in the Foundation Stage (Second Edition)
London: David Fulton Publishers

Themed Days

Sparkly Day

What you need:

▶ a selection of sparkly objects: CDs, mirrors, fairy lights, costume jewellery etc.

▶ tin foil, tinsel and glitter

▶ a dark or mirrored surface for displaying and making patterns on or a large area covered with tin foil

▶ magnifying glasses

▶ a camera/camcorder

What you do:

1. Prior to your Sparkly Day ask children to bring in a sparkly item from home, e.g. a piece of costume jewllery.

2. Decorate your setting with the tinsel and other sparkly materials.

3. Make a huge group display or smaller individual ones of the sparkly items that you and the children have brought in. A display looks particularly effective on a mirrored table or large pieces of safety mirror. Try completely covering a table with tin foil if you don't have mirrored surfaces.

4. Let the children explore and talk about all the sparkly items. Encourage them to look at the objects in detail – taking photographs of their favourite things or looking at them through magnifying glasses.

5. Sort the objects into groups: silver, gold, multicoloured, etc.

6. Talk about all of the words they could use to describe the sparkly things and make up a group poem.

Ready for more?

▶ Add sparkly things to your water tray – use tongs to pick up the items.

▶ Try adding glitter to playdough, sand etc.

▶ Make shiny paintings by mixing icing sugar and water. Paint the mixture over paper and then add drops of food colouring – see how shiny it is when it dries!

▶ Try hanging a selection of shiny mobiles in an area with fairy lights and mirrors – how do the children feel? What words do they use? Let the children spend lots of time here if they wish, just watching the different colours and sparkly reflections in the mirrors. If you have not got safety mirrors, reflective paper or mirror tiles are just as exciting.

and more?

▶ Decorate unwanted CDs with glitter and sequins. When dry, try covering a complete wall with the CDs – the end result is extremely sparkly especially if it is an outdoor sunny wall!

▶ Try looking at kaleidoscopes – look out for the ones that have sparkly patterns – the children love watching the changing patterns.

▶ Give each child a shoebox covered in tin foil. Let the children stick a few sparkly items onto the box to make their own 'Sparkle Box'. If the box is laid on its side it can be fixed to a wall (stapled or double sided tape) with lots of other boxes to make a sparkly wall. Try arranging fairy lights around them to really set off your wall!

▶ Try painting objects in PVA – plastic pots, shapes, unwanted keys, CDs etc. and then coating them in glitter. Hang them from canes to make sparkly mobiles.

Links to the Early Learning Goals

PD: 7, 8	PSED: 1, 2, 4, 8
CLL: 1, 2, 6	PSRN: 9, 12
KUW: 1, 5, 6, 7	CD: 2, 3, 5

Dinosaur Day

What you need:

- large plastic dinosaurs
- small world dinosaurs
- paper cups
- sand
- Plaster of Paris

- a camera/camcorder
- a tuff spot
- toothbrushes
- small paint/glue/make-up brushes
- magnifying glasses

What you do:

1. In advance, fill the paper cups about half way with damp sand.

2. Use the large dinosaurs to make footprints in the damp sand.

3. Pour the Plaster of Paris over each footprint and leave to dry.

4. When the plaster is dry carefully peel away the paper cups.

5. Place the plaster 'fossils' on a display table or in a tuff spot with more sand and small world dinosaurs around them.

6. Let the children enjoy free play.

Don't worry if there is sand left on the plaster! Add brushes and magnifying glasses to the table so the children can brush the sand off the fossils.

Ready for more?

▶ Dinosaur Dominoes/Dinosaur Snap – make your own cards from clip art or from dinosaur gift paper. Glue the pictures onto stiff card and laminate.

▶ Dinosaur Biscuits – use dinosaur-shaped pastry cutters and decorate with icing.

▶ Dinosaur Models from junk materials – use models, pictures, books, the internet for inspiration. See how large you can make the models.

▶ Dinosaur Hunt – indoors or outdoors. Hide as many small world dinosaurs as possible around your setting. If you haven't got enough dinosaurs, photocopy lots of dinosaur pictures and laminate them. Give each child a bag or container to collect them in. How many can they recognise and name?

and more?

▶ Dinosaur Egg – Find a very large stone, the bigger the better. Clean it up and place it somewhere where the children will spot it. Let them think it is a dinosaur egg and encourage them to use their imaginations! The children will be fascinated – find pictures and look for information together. When the children are busy with another dinosaur activity, make some marks on the pretend egg using felt tip pen to suggest that the egg is starting to hatch. How do the children react? What has happened? What will happen next? Make a book about the 'Mystery Egg' using photographs, children's drawings, their comments etc. When you feel that the time is right for the egg to hatch you can leave some baby dinosaurs in its place. Tell the children that the egg had to be taken away but the other dinosaurs were so pleased with how the children had looked after it that they left the baby dinosaurs as a 'thank you'. (Remember to keep the large stone well out of sight after this activity or the magic might just be spoiled!)

Links to the Early Learning Goals

KUW: 1, 2, 3, 5, 6, 7

CD: 1, 2, 3, 5

PSED: 1, 2, 3

PSRN: 1, 2, 3, 6, 9, 12

CLL: 1, 2, 3, 4, 5, 7, 8

PD: 8

Teddy Bear Day

An opportunity for everyone to bring their favourite bear into nursery!

What you need:

▶ ask every child to bring a bear to the setting (have some spares available)

▶ collection of old bears or pictures of old bears for the children to look at

▶ stories about bears e.g. 'Goldilocks' or 'We're Going on a Bear Hunt'

I will need

What you do:

Teddy bear circle time

Encourage everyone to sit in a circle with their bear. Ask each
child to introduce their bear and tell the group something about him/her.
There are opportunities here for names, colours, where the bear came from etc.
Ask children to look around the circle. Who has the biggest bear? The smallest?
Who has a white bear? A black bear? Whose bear is wearing clothes?

Bear books

Read 'Goldilocks and the three bears' and 'We're going on a bear hunt'. Act them
out. Use the visiting teddies as part of the action!

CD bear

Provide an old CD for each child which will be the bear's face. Look at pictures of
bears together, and talk about what they will need for their bear's face. CDs can
be painted or fabric stuck on them for fur and ears. Facial features can be drawn,
painted or stuck on.

Teddy bear picnic

Take the bears outside and have a picnic lunch if the weather is dry enough.
Alternatively, have a picnic on tablecloths laid out on the floor inside.

Ready for more?

▶ Bear Responsibilities – use Teddy Bear Day to remind the children of the
importance of being a good friend. Today, bear is the new friend and
they will have to show him how to do everything, where everything is
and what there is to do that's exciting in nursery.

Links to the Early Learning Goals

PSED: 1, 2, 3, 4, 7, 8, 12
CLL: 1, 2, 3, 4, 5, 6, 7, 8, 17
PSRN: 1, 2, 3, 4, 9, 12

KUW: 1, 2, 3, 4, 7, 8
PD: 1, 2, 4, 7
CD: 1, 2, 3, 5

Bike Day

What you need:

- a large safe area (playground, outdoor area)
- a selection of bikes (three and four wheelers and bikes with stabilisers for the younger children)
- extra adults (to supervise)
- safety helmets
- cones or markers
- a 'pedestrian crossing'
- a number of milk crates
- chalk
- a whistle
- a camera or camcorder (to record the event)

I will need

What you do:

Prior to the day:

1. Explain to the children that they are invited to bring in their bikes for the day. Try to acquire a few spare bikes for those who do not own one. (If there are children without bikes, get them to sit and watch and cheer for their friends whilst they wait for their go!)

2. Send letters home to parents/carers explaining that it will be a special 'Bike Day'. Invite parents/carers to come along – some might be able to bring their bikes or help supervise. Remind parents that **ALL** children (and adults!) must have a safety helmet and that all bikes and helmets must be named.

3. Decide where bikes are to go when children first arrive – maybe have a registration desk – a space will be needed!

4. Decide where the cycling is to take place – the obvious area is a playground. Before 'Bike Day', have a good look around to check that it is safe – you might want to cordon off an area. Make sure you will be able to see all your little cyclists at all times.

Setting up an obstacle course:

1. Well before your cyclists arrive set up the obstacle course. Make sure all of the cyclists travel in one direction (very important to avoid collisions!). Mark out a 'road' with the cones, markers, chalks etc. Make roundabouts using the milk crates placed in a circle. Have a 'pedestrian crossing' where they have to stop, and place red, green and orange markers where they have to 'stop', 'go', 'get ready to go'.

2. Set up a base where children can stop for a rest and a drink.

3. Before the children set off on the course make sure they know that when you blow the whistle they need to stop and return to their base.

4. Talk about the safety issues and why it is important to wear a helmet and what bells and brakes are used for!

5. At the end of their time on the obstacle course present the children and adults with a certificate. Have a little ceremony – don't forget to take some photographs!

Ready for more?

▶ Look at and talk about the children's bikes. Are there any the same? Look at colours, sizes, wheels, pedals, bells, horns, seats etc. See if the children can arrange the bikes in order of size. How many bikes are there? How many have 2 wheels, 3 wheels, 4 wheels?

▶ Have a 'Treasure Hunt' on bikes. Hide things around the outdoor area – shapes, ribbons, balls etc. Each child needs a bag on their bike to collect their treasure in. Think about tying your Treasure Hunt in with a topic – collecting Easter Egg cut-outs, autumn leaves, coloured items, dinosaur pictures etc. For older children you can place written clues around your outdoor area which they have to work out before cycling to the next clue.

▶ Look at the different patterns tyres make. Try putting down long pieces of wallpaper (plain side up), roll paint onto the beginning of the piece and let the children cycle through it. What do they notice about the various marks? (Don't be tempted to use thinner paper as it will tear very easily.) Try also opening out large cardboard boxes to cycle over.

Links to the Early Learning Goals

PD: 2, 4, 5, 6, 7   PSRN: 1, 2, 3, 9, 12
KUW: 1, 2, 3, 4, 8   CLL: 3, 5, 6
PSED: 2, 4, 8

Ribbon Day

What you need:

▶ a huge selection of ribbons of different colours, widths and lengths (Make sure they aren't too long or children will step on them and not be able to move easily.)

▶ CD player

▶ CDs of lively music that is good to move to

▶ a space to move and dance – indoors or outdoors

▶ cameras and camcorders

Saftey warning: When using ribbons, children should be supervised at all times to avoid the dangers of tangling or inappropriate behaviour.

What you do:

1. Put the ribbons in a container easily accessible to children and ask them to choose one or two each.

2. Explain to children that they are 'special dancing ribbons' that move to music.

3. Encourage children to help you operate the CD player and choose a CD. Ask them about their choice of music and of ribbon/ribbons.

4. When the music starts show the children how to make the ribbons dance – high, low, up, down, fast, slow, circling, swirling, tiptoeing, bouncing, shaking.

5. Encourage the children to describe the way their dancing ribbons are moving to the music. Encourage them to listen to the music – is it fast, slow, happy, sad?

6. If you have access to full length safety mirrors children can observe their own ribbon dancing. Or encourage children to use cameras or camcorders to record each other so that they can play back their dances and look at the moves they made.

Ready for more?

▶ Ribbon Trails – Using longer lengths of ribbon, tie anything you like to the end of the ribbon – numbers, letters, dinosaurs, a special letter etc. (You might link to this to a topic you are already exploring.) Trail the ribbon around things and not just in a straight line so that children have to actually follow the shape of the trail. If you do this outdoors on a playground or field you can use string or rope. When the children find the surprise at the end of the trail ask them how they found it, what did they have to do? Then let them make their own trails.

▶ Ribbon Pictures/Ribbon Collages – Using a large selection of ribbons of various lengths. See what pictures and patterns can be created. Use large spaces indoors and out – the children can work in a group or independently. For smaller pieces of work they can glue their ribbons onto paper/fabric etc. Try joining lots of individual ribbon collages together for a striking effect.

- ▶ Ribbon Threading/Weaving – Have a large group weaving activity using garden trellis. Offer lots of different types of ribbons. Tie it in with the Seasons (e.g. autumn colours etc) or a topic (e.g. silver and blue ribbons for a snowy feel). See The Little Book of Sewing and Weaving for more ideas.

- ▶ Ribbon Lucky Dip – Place items in a container which are attached to different coloured ribbons. Have things such as a bunch of keys, plastic numbers, plastic letters, small world plastic animals. Place them around the container with the ribbon hanging over the side and fill the container with sawdust or even shredded paper. The children choose a ribbon, talk about what they think may be attached to it and then talk about what it actually is. Encourage them to take turns.

- ▶ Maypole Dancing – Place a tall garden cane in a tub or bucket and fill with sand or stone chippings to hold it secure. Tie or stick about 4-6 different coloured ribbons to the top of the cane. Children can skip around the cane to music watching how the ribbons wind around and make a pattern. Older children can try more adventurous dancing.

Links to the Early Learning Goals

PD: 1, 2, 4, 8   KUW: 7
CLL: 3, 5, 8   PSED: 1, 2, 4, 8
CD: 1, 2, 3, 4, 5   PSRN: 1, 3

23

Fairy Day

What you need:

▶ a tiny 'fairy' door (made of clay or card) fixed to your skirting board

▶ fairy pictures or small world fairies

▶ fairy dust (glitter)

▶ 'fairy' writing paper

I will need

What you do:

1. Tell the children about the fairy living in your setting and how it flies about at night and sometimes leaves little gifts or messages.

2. Show them the door so they know where the magical area is. To make it more special, place little fairy pictures or small world fairies and twinkling lights around the area.

3. Sprinkle the fairy dust (glitter) around the little door – you can make a trail that leads to shapes, numbers, letters etc and tell the children that the fairy did it. Or try sprinkling the glitter in the shape of a number, letter or shape. The children will know if the fairy has visited when they spot the fairy dust signs.

4. Provide special paper with fairy pictures on or with a fairy border to encourage mark making/writing to the fairies. The fairy can become their little penpal and leave letters or messages for the children to read.

Ready for more?

▶ Encourage physical and creative development by making wings and fairy clothes from floaty material – the children will love using their imaginations, dancing and moving to magical fairy music.

▶ Look at musical instruments and explore which sounds would be best for fairy music.

Links to the Early Learning Goals

CD: 2, 5   PSED: 1, 8
CLL: 2, 4, 7, 17   PD: 1, 7, 8
PSRN: 2, 3, 12

Construction Day

What you need:

▶ Indoor construction materials: cardboard boxes and tubes, string, sellotape, hole punches, scissors, split pins, elastic bands, masking tape, staplers, pegs, fabric and paper.

▶ Small world construction: Duplo, Lego, Sticklebrix, Mobilo, Block Play, Mega Blocks, Wedgitts, Magnetix, Gears, Popoids, etc.

▶ Outdoor constuction materials: planks, crates, large boxes, guttering, tyres, very large card, carpet tubes, string, rope, pegs, plastic tubing, fabric, sheets, tarpaulin, shower curtains, garden canes, garden trellis, logs, buckets, large tubs.

▶ Cameras and camcorders

What you do:

1. Set out as many of the above materials as possible in your inside and outside areas. Give the children plenty of space to work in.

2. Make sure the children know where the tools and equipment are set out and also **remind them about safety rules** and replacing tools after use. You could set up a 'tool and equipment station' so everyone knows where things are.

3. Encourage the children to look at the wide range of materials on offer and talk about what they would like to construct.

4. Get the children to think about what they need to join pieces together – encourage independence but be there to assist with tricky tasks.

5. When children have made their constructions have a special place where they can be displayed – their own special gallery! Invite parents and other children to look at their work.

6. Remember to have cameras and camcorders available for children and staff to record their work (and the process – not just the end result).

Ready for more?

▶ If your setting is part of a school why not invite a few classes to take part in a 'Constructathon'? The older children will inspire and even help the younger ones.

▶ Invite parents to join in with the constructions – their knowledge will be invaluable and the quality time together will be enjoyed by all.

Links to the Early Learning Goals

PD: 7, 8	PSED: 1, 2, 4, 8
CLL: 1, 2, 6	PSRN: 9, 12
KUW: 1, 5, 6, 7	CD: 2, 3, 5

Minibeasts Day

The subject of minibeasts is very popular and diverse. A day is hardly long enough to explore all the opportunities! It will however prompt some thoughts and interest from the children and you may then be able to take their learning forward in the direction they are most interested in.

What you need:

▶ large and small washable minibeast models (plastic or rubber)
▶ paper, pencils and clipboards
▶ cameras
▶ magnifying glasses
▶ bug catcher pots
▶ paints
▶ scissors
▶ foam and wooden objects to print with
▶ collection of books about minibeasts (fiction and non-fiction)
▶ some minibeast rhymes/songs

What you do:

1. Have a minibeast hunt! Prior to the hunt, collect pictures of minibeasts and arrange on an A4 sized piece of paper. Photocopy as many copies as you need for every child. Dependent on the number of beasts you have you may need 4 or 5 A4 sheets so that they are well spaced out.

2. When you have your sheets ready, cut each minibeast out, then laminate the original set of minibeasts and hide them or stick them around the nursery and outdoor area.

3. Give each child a clipboard, one of the photocopied sheets and a pencil. Then send them off to detect where the minibeasts are hidden!

4. As the children find the minibeasts they can tick or mark them on the sheet. The children may work alone or in pairs/groups.

5. Take photographs as they look at each minibeast and see if it matches one on their sheet!

Ready for more?

▶ More minibeast hunting – Let the children go on a real minibeast hunt in either your outdoor area or a safe area nearby. They will need magnifying glasses, cameras and bug catcher pots. Encourage children to think about where they might find the bugs and why. If they want to handle them, remind them about being careful and gentle. Some may want to use the magnifiers to just look at the bugs. Take pencils and paper with you for on the spot observational drawing.

▶ Book task – Using any available minibeast books, ask the children to find a picture of a butterfly, a worm, a beetle etc. If they manage that, make it harder by asking for a butterfly on a flower or a cocoon.

and more?

Butterfly painting – Fold a piece of paper in half, then open it up. Get the child to paint or make patterns on only one side of the fold. Then fold the paper, press, open up and you have a symmetrical pattern! When dry, cut out in a butterfly shape. Alternatively let the children cut out a symmetrical butterfly shape prior to painting.

Insect prints – Put some paint of various colours in shallow trays and add items that can be printed with, in various shapes: you could use sponges, wooden blocks etc. Talk to the children about the shape of an insect, and then see if they can use the blocks and sponges to print their own insect creation.

Links to the Early Learning Goals

PSED: 1, 2, 3, 4, 7, 8, 9, 12
CLL: 1, 2, 3, 4, 5, 7, 8, 17

Football Day

What you need:

▶ white card, paper and paper plates
▶ paint and pens
▶ ribbon
▶ black wool/string
▶ single hole punch
▶ sellotape
▶ straws/thin canes
▶ scissors

What you do:

Decorate your setting with the following ideas:

1. Let the children handprint all over a large piece of paper using the colours of their favourite team. Cut the dry handprints out. Cut out the centre of a paper plate, leaving the outside 'O' shape. Arrange handprints around the edge. Add ribbon in a team colour as a tag to hang.

2. Use the internet/books to look at team flags. Then let the children make their own flag! Use paper for the flag, pens or paints to decorate and then sellotape the flag to straws or thin pieces of cane. Then display all over your setting!

3. Cut out some triangular shaped pieces of paper and let the children decorate them in their team's colours. Punch holes in the bottom edge and thread string through to create a long line of triangles, making a banner.

Ready for more?

▶ Matching Sock Game – Collect as many pairs of football socks as you can! Jumble them up and see if the children can find a matching pair! Talk about colours, patterns, teams. Count how many pairs you have! Alternatively, you could play this game with football tops. With the tops, look at what is the same and what is different (colours, numbers, patterns, teams) rather than matching pairs.

▶ If possible borrow a football table and have a five-a-side indoor championship! If you don't have access to a football table you can use an ordinary table. Attach card around the edge of the table to stop the ball going off. Cover the table with paper (stuck down) and then mark up a football pitch. Make goal posts out of lollipop sticks or pipe cleaners. For the players, use whatever you can to make up your teams of 5 – 5 animals, 5 dolls, 5 small world people. Make sure someone has an individual whiteboard or notebook to keep score!

and more?

▶ Borrow or buy a cheap inflatable goal for football practice! Talk about why exercise is good for you and what happens to your body when you exercise.

▶ Look at books about football and football teams, or watch some football online/DVD.

▶ Whilst it is the taking part that matters, not the winning, perhaps the children could look at pictures of football trophies and make their own to give their friends when they have done well scoring goals or when they have played on the football table.

Links to the Early Learning Goals

PSED: 1, 2, 3, 4, 5, 7, 8, 9, 11, 12

Fruit and Vegetable Day

Important: Check at the outset for any allergies to fruits or vegetables. Remember to prompt lots of hand washing before eating!

What you need:

- examples of as many different fruits and vegetables that are in season (or your local supermarket has available)
- books depicting fruit and vegetables
- a sharp knife (adult use only)
- cups and plates
- paper and paint

- shallow trays and sponges
- a camera
- magnifying glasses
- seeds and pots
- ice lolly molds
- a blender
- skewers

I will need

What you do:

1. Place a wide selection of fruit and vegetables on a table so that children can look at them at touch them.

2. Encourage words suggesting texture and colour and shape. Do any of them smell?

3. Slice fruit and vegetables so that the children can look at them with magnifying glasses. Offer paper and pencils for observational drawings. Let the children take close up photographs of the fruit and vegetables and once printed see who can identify and name them.

Ready for more?

▶ Fruit and Vegetable Printing

1. Slice a variety of fruits and vegetables – some down the middle, some lengthways – so that the children can look at the patterns inside. Look to see if they are the same on each side.

2. Children paint the flat cut side of the fruit/vegetable and then to place this down on paper. When it is pressed lightly it should leave its shape. Alternatively, pour paint into a shallow tray and then place a sponge into the bottom of the tray. By pressing the sponge down the paint will seep into it and then you can push the fruit or vegetable into the sponge to get the cut edge covered in paint. Once again press this lightly down on paper to create a print.

3. Some vegetables such as carrots, red cabbage and beetroot – if sliced thinly and then boiled and strained – will leave their 'dye' behind and the children can then use this to paint with or to stain materials such as cotton.

▶ Mr Potato Head – Give each child a potato and let them, where possible, scoop the top of it out. Then sprinkle with mustard or cress seeds! Watch, over the coming days, his hair begin to grow! Alternatively, decorate a yoghurt pot with a face and place cotton wool inside. Moisten the cotton wool and then sprinkle with mustard or cress seeds. Again, watch that hair grow!

and more?

▶ Grow Your Own – Where possible grow your own vegetables in your outdoor area. Potatoes, beans and snap peas are very easy to grow and maintain in pots or bags if you have no ground available to plant in. There is nothing that compares to a child seeing their plant coming out of the ground!

▶ Snack Attack – Make sure all snacks available are fruit and vegetables on this special day! Arrange them in colours, make smiley faces from them. Show the children these food groups are fun!

▶ Fruit Smoothies – Using a blender and low fat natural yoghurt, add fruit and blend to make smoothies for the children who might not think they like fruit.

▶ Fruit Kebabs – Dice various fruits and then let the children load their own choices onto the skewers! Are all fruits the same colour when diced up? Try a VEGETABLE KEBAB. These can be eaten raw or cooked!

▶ Fruit Ice Lollies – Blend together vanilla yoghurt, pineapple juice and small pieces of fruit. Once blended pour into lolly molds and freeze! Eat when solid.

Links to the Early Learning Goals

PSED: 1, 2, 4, 8, 12

CLL: 1, 2, 3, 4, 7, 8, 17

PSRN: 1, 2, 3, 4, 10, 11, 12

KUW: 1, 2, 3, 7

PD: 1, 2, 7

CD: 1, 2, 3, 5

Music Day

Streamer Plate Shaker

What you need:

- paper plates
- poster paints and paintbrushes
- PVA glue
- rice, dried beans or beads
- strips of tissue paper/crêpe paper or fabric

- a stapler and scissors
- aprons
- table covering

What you do:

1. Paint the bottom of the paper plate and leave to dry.
2. Cut thin strips of tissue paper/crêpe paper/fabric.
3. Glue one end of the inside of the paper plate. Stick several strips of tissue paper on until you have covered half of the plate. Let it dry thoroughly.
4. Fold the paper plate in half, painted side out.
5. Place a handful of rice/beads/beans inside the folded plate and then staple the sides together – all around the edge so that the contents cannot fall out.
6. Now, shake, shake, shake!

Drum
What you need:

- a round tub/bucket
- a piece of strong plastic or opened out carrier bag/bin liner
- elastic bands
- poster paints
- PVA Glue
- brushes or glue stickers
- sequins/glitter/stickers
- aprons
- table covering

What you do:

1. Cut a circle out of the plastic which is 2–3 inches larger in diameter than the top of your tub/bucket.

2. Place the plastic on top of the tub/bucket and pull it tight whilst securing with elastic bands. Make sure it is really taut.

3. Now decorate the sides of the drum. Add PVA glue to the paint so that it doesn't peel off. Use the stickers and sequins to add sparkle to the drum.

4. Play, using hands.

Jingle Bell Mitts
What you need:

- large pieces of felt
- jingle bells
- PVA or strong glue
- brushes or glue sticks
- a needle and thread
- aprons
- table covering

What you do:

1. Cut 4 oversized mitten shapes out of felt.
2. Take 2 matching mitts and attach together with glue or sew together.
3. Repeat with another 2 pieces of felt.
4. Sew 4 jingle bells along the finger edge of each mitt.
5. Slip on and shake and clap hands together to make music!

Tube Maracas

What you need:

- a cardboard tube (from tin foil, cling film, kitchen or toilet paper roll)
- wide sticky tape
- dried rice
- stickers/paint/felt pens
- ribbons

What you do:

1. Stick a few pieces of tape across one end of the tube, leaving no gaps.

2. Put a few handfuls of rice in the tube – some will stick to the tape.

3. Stick a few pieces of tape across the open end of the tube, again making sure not to leave any gaps for rice to fall through!

4. Decorate your maraca – draw and paint patterns on it and tie long ribbons around it.

Ready for more?

- Invite musically talented staff or parents to come in and play and talk about their musical instrument to the children.

- Let the children express themselves with dance or play musical games such as musical chairs or musical statues.

- Musical Painting – have a selection of music to play whilst the children are painting. Can they interpret the music through their painting? Is it fast/slow/happy/sad?

Links to the Early Learning Goals

PD: 1, 2, 4, 8
CLL: 3, 4, 5, 8
PSED: 1, 2

KUW: 1, 2, 4, 5, 6, 7
CD: 1, 2, 3, 4, 5

Wet, Wet, Wet Day!

What you need:

▶ waterproof trousers and jackets and wellies
▶ a large water tray or a cheap paddling pool
▶ ramps, chutes, pipes, guttering – different sizes
▶ a hose
▶ a selection of funnels
▶ plastic jugs, bottles, containers and buckets

What you do:

1. Fill the water tray or paddling pool up – a garden hose is useful as the children will quickly use up the water and will want the tray refilled!

2. Fit the guttering together to make a really long water channel. Extend the various ramps, chutes etc all over your outdoor area so children can see just how far water will travel.

3. Suspend some of the pipes or chutes at child height to add interest – provide a sturdy, wide-based stool for children to reach the suspended channels and watch the water going through them.

4. Let the children rearrange the plastic pipes, thinking and working together to move equipment safely, make correct links and work out why the water runs through some channels and not others?

Ready for more?

▶ Fix a really long piece of transparent hose to your outdoor fence or wall. Start off high and trail and secure it – string or masking tape will normally do the trick. Can the children carefully carry a container of water, pour it down the hose and watch it on its' journey?

▶ Suspended sieves, funnels, and small buckets are good fun over a large water tray and give the children plenty to think about. Try putting holes in some plastic containers and not in others – what is happening and why? Try putting different sized holes in containers – again, what is happening and why?

▶ Fill as many small containers – plastic bowls, ice cream pots, ice cube trays – with water and freeze the day before. The children can help. Ask children if they know why you are putting them in the freezer? What will happen? How will you get the ice out of the containers? What shape will it be? Add the ice to your water tray or paddling pool. The children will have to be very careful with the ice – explain about only using tools such as spoons, sticks and tongs to touch the ice. Add small world arctic animals. Children can move the animals over the ice – retrieving them from very icy water using tongs or nets.

41

And more?

▶ Small World Play in your water tray – think about small world people and animals with rafts and boats. Children can count, sort, as well as think about making jetties for small world people to get on boats.

▶ Soapy Sponges – Let the children squirt some washing up liquid into the water tray. They are going to see if they can change the water by just using the sponges. This activity is really good for strengthening little fingers and hands as the children will really have to squeeze those sponges to produce lots of lather! What is happening to the water? What is happening to the sponges? Who has the heaviest sponge? Why? Where is all of the water? How can you get the water out of the sponge? Does your sponge weigh the same now? Let the children also use their very lathery sponges on smooth surfaces like plastic tables or a spread out shower curtain and encourage them to mark make on these large surfaces using fingers, hands, sticks, brushes, wheels of cars – anything! Then, wipe over the surface with their soapy sponge and start again!

Links to the Early Learning Goals

PD: 4, 7, 8

CLL: 1, 2, 3, 5, 7

PSED: 1, 2, 8

PSRN: 1, 2, 3, 11, 12

KUW: 1, 2, 3, 6, 7

CD: 1, 3, 5

Charity Day

General guidelines for organising a charity day in your setting:

Many schools and nurseries take on board a charity for a year, and then raise money specifically to give to that cause. This is a good way to unite a school to work towards one main aim. However, at times, personal matters occur such as a child having a serious illness/disability and then as a community it is great if school and nursery can show support for the parent and their needs. Alternatively a nursery may want to fundraise for a national or international campaign such as Red Nose Day or Children in Need.

Prior to any event it is a good idea to talk with the children about the charity or the area you want to support and why. Ask them what they could do to help and why we need to help others.

Decide if your setting is going to run one big event or whether there will be various fundraisers going on during that day.

Prior to the event send out sponsor forms that indicate what you are trying to raise money for. For some parents with little money themselves and no work colleagues or family to ask for sponsorship this can be financially difficult. On the letter make sure that parents are aware that any amount, however small will help, and a small donation can be given rather than sponsorship if necessary.

Make sure that at the end of the session or day, each child takes home a certificate (photocopiable) that congratulates them and says they completed the charity event!

Once the money comes in, don't forget to thank parents and let them know the running total. Keep it at the forefront of conversation so those who are slower at getting the money in will be prompted to do so!

The following ideas will suit a nursery setting but can be modified to suit the age group you are working with. Think about organising an event that your children will succeed at and enjoy! Where children are involved lots of praise and encouragement is needed and an emphasis on the taking part being the important part of a charity day or event.

What you need:

▶ a day set aside specifically for the event(s) you choose
▶ a camera/camcorder to capture the event

Ideas:

Bad hair day: A quick and easy way to raise money! Charge everyone 50p/£1 to come to the setting with 'bad' hair! Staff too!

Own clothes/Fancy dress day: Once again charge a set price to come to the setting in fancy dress (or own clothes if a uniform is usually worn).

Sponsored bike ride: This event does not take long so maybe use the older children's playground to add some excitement! Mark out a simple circular or rectangular shape that the children have to ride around. Please see 'Bike Day' on page 18 for more details on how to set up an obstacle course and safety issues. The sponsored amount of times around the 'course' should be very doable, e.g. 3 laps. Encourage parents to come and watch and cheer for the children. You need to make sure EVERYONE can succeed! If the weather is kind and the support from parents good, why not have drinks outside after the event?

Cake bake sale: Ask each child to bring from home some sort of baked goods, e.g. cakes, scones, flapjacks, and then sell them at the end of the session or at the end of the day.

Book sale: Ask for donations of books from children, their families and staff and hold a book sale.

Face painting: Invite a talented parent/staff member to paint faces but charge 50p a time!

Raffles: Start collecting prizes/donations well before you want to hold the raffle so that you have lots of prizes on offer. Sell tickets, and do the prize giving as an event on its own or at the end of a big day of fundraising.

Welly throwing competion: As it says in the title. Challenge the children to have a go. Measure the distance and at the end of the event, offer a prize for the furthest throw.

Jelly welly walking: Fill two oversized wellies (adult sized) with set jelly. Get sponsorship for children to walk a certain distance in the filled wellies!

Funny photo competiton: Pay £1 to enter a photograph and then let the rest of the group decide which is the funniest. Offer a small prize for the owner of the funniest photograph!

Links to the Early Learning Goals

Learning Areas will be dependent on the ideas you decide to use.

Snowy Day

What you need:

- snow!
- warm weatherproof clothes
- spare wellies so that everyone can join in
- mark making tools – sticks, pebbles, small wheels etc.
- a tuff spot (builders' plastic tray)
- small plastic containers, bowls and spoons

What you do:

1. Make sure everyone is well wrapped up.

2. Offer a selection of mark making tools, bowls and spoons and whatever else the children would like to use and encourage them to enjoy free, creative play in the snow.

3. Keep children moving around with active games such as dancing in the snow, making snowmen, 'Who can throw the furthest snowball?' competition and 'Follow the leader'.

4. Make snow pictures using cones, leaves, conkers, pieces of string, rope etc.

Ready for more?

▶ Under supervision, and for short periods only (due to cold hands), let the children paint on the snow – dropping liquid paints or food colouring (try using pipettes or spoons). Watch what happens to their paintings over a few days as the snow melts or more snow falls.

▶ Hide numbers, letters, shapes, coloured objects in the snow and have a treasure hunt!

Links to the Early Learning Goals

KUW: 1, 3   CLL: 1, 5
CD: 1, 3   PSED:1, 2
PD: 1, 7, 8

Congratulations Day

Congratulations Day can take place at any time, but a focus could be for end of term or end of nursery/reception year. It is a day when every child receives congratulations for something they have done. These wishes do not have to be for academic goals achieved they could be for trying, for being kind or helpful. You can make the day about what is important in your setting.

Invite parents to your setting at the end or beginning of a session to watch as their child receives acknowledgement from the staff.

What you need:

- ▶ banners
- ▶ balloons
- ▶ streamers
- ▶ certificates/scrolls (possibly laminated)
- ▶ a camera to capture the moment
- ▶ someone to present the awards

What you do:

1. Inform parents as early as possible of the up-and-coming event so those that work can make arrangements to be there. Send out letters, add to web pages and put on the newsletters.

2. Organise for someone special to present the certificates. This could be the Head or a Governor (if the children know them), or maybe even their next teacher if they are moving up into school.

3. Let the children make banners and streamers and paper chains to decorate the setting. Blow up balloons and arrange seating for parents.

4. Someone needs to give a speech at the start that talks about each child being unique and having special gifts to offer, and then a swift 'ceremony' where each child has their accomplishments read out and their certificate presented to them.

5. When every child has received their award, large amounts of praise and clapping are necessary!

6. Add to the occasion by getting your children to sing a few songs, play instruments, show work that has been done, etc.

Ready for more?

▶ This celebration could be made more formal by having in the hall or a local church.

▶ If you have the space perhaps offer tea, coffee and biscuits to parents.

Links to the Early Learning Goals

KUW: 8, 10   PSED: 2
CLL: 5, 8, 17, 19   PSRN: 1, 3, 12
PD: 8   CD: 2, 5

Moving House Day

Moving house is a big event for a child. If a child in your setting is moving house, help them to talk about and enjoy their move with the following activities.

What you need:

- ▶ doll's house and furniture
- ▶ boxes to make dolls' houses
- ▶ small world trucks and lorries
- ▶ number stickers, foam numbers, magnetic numbers
- ▶ cardboard strips for road signs
- ▶ new home cards – bought or handmade
- ▶ new home 'presents' (boxes wrapped in gift paper and artificial flowers)
- ▶ change of address announcement cards – bought or handmade

What you do:

1. Prior to the day, find out as much information about the move as possible from the parents – the address, photo of new home, moving date, etc.

2. Talk to the rest of the children about their friend moving house.

3. Offer small world houses and boxes for children to make their own homes. Which bedroom will they be sleeping in? Do they have a garden, garage etc?

4. Let the children decorate their little home – making the front door the same colour as their new door will be (if they know it). Provide numbers for them to stick on to their house.

5. Talk about where it is – street names etc. Make road signs from cardboard strips.

6. Talk about how people let friends know about the move. Show children 'New Home' or 'We're Moving' cards. Let them make their own.

7. Look at 'New Home' cards – why do people send them? Think about new home presents.

8. Talk about keeping in touch with friends and making new ones.

Ready for more?

▶ Talk about how people move their furniture and belongings to a new home. Provide small world trucks and vans for children to act out the move.

▶ How will people find their way to their new home? Look at street maps (or make your own), think about directions and SAT Nav/GPS systems.

Links to the Early Learning Goals

These will depend on the type of achievements your setting places the greatest onus on.

Parent's Day

Many settings work closely in partnership with parents nowadays, but this isn't the case everywhere! Have a special day for those parents who are unable to work as closely with you as they would like to because of work or other commitments.

Why not choose a date and make 'Parent's Day' an annual event in your setting!

What you need:

▶ parents!
▶ the setting equipped for lots of activities indoors and outdoors!
▶ cameras to capture the day

What you do:

1. Prior to the day, ensure all parents are invited to the special day well in advance.

2. Have a general plan for your 'Parent's Day' which is flexible and adaptable. Activities should be available to cover every area of learning and staff should be available to talk to parents about the learning that can be gained from whatever is out. Whilst your main aim may be for the parents and children to spend time together, for some an opportunity to talk to other parents may benefit them greatly!

3. Parents should be encouraged (and this will mean gently for some) to play with their child, to paint, to use clay, and to build.

4. Encourage parents to stay as long as they wish, and organise lunch/café time to support this (e.g. make sure extra fruit/snacks are available and space available for parents to eat their packed lunch or to stay for a cooked lunch).

5. Come together at various points during the day – maybe for storytime or singing and rhymes?

Ready for more?

▶ If you have children from a culture different from that of the majority, maybe Parent's Day could include something multicultural for everyone to gain an understanding of a background different from their own. Use the day to bring everyone together!

Links to the Early Learning Goals

The learning areas covered will vary depending on the type of day you provide.

Grandparent's Day

Children love to 'show off' their grandparents – and why not? Remember those who may not be fortunate enough to have any – be sure to let them invite somebody just as special.

What you need:

▶ as many grandparents or special visitors as possible

▶ a special table – beautifully decorated with flowers

▶ cakes and biscuits (some made in advance by children)

▶ cold drinks (unless there is a safe area for tea/coffee)

▶ a CD player and CDs of grandparents' choice

▶ memorabilia – sent in advance and named

▶ camera, camcorder

▶ photos of grandparents/special people and of child they're linked to

▶ enough seats for everyone

What you do:

1. Decide well in advance the date of this special day. Children make invitations to their grandparents – inviting them in because they are 'special'. Explain in a separate letter to grandparents that you would love them to share their childhood/young adult memories with the children and staff. (Make sure you ask for replies to help with your preparations.)

2. Ask grandparents to send in any photographs/memorabilia in advance to put on display. Also ask for any photographs of them with their grandchildren. You could ask them to fill in a simple questionnaire about their hobbies when they were younger, what they played with etc. These answers could be displayed alongside the answers of their grandchildren to the same questions. You could also include the photographs.

3. Make the day really special. Maybe the children could make big flowers to arrange around the entrance area along with a big sign or banner saying 'Grandparent's Day' or 'Welcome Special People'. Put up balloons and streamers.

4. Make the special table look wonderful, with the help of the children, all the while talking to the children about why they are celebrating.

5. If you have somebody who is particularly good at baking, you could suggest they make a cake.

6. Ask the children why these people are special to them and write down their answers on large pieces of card/paper to display with the relevant photographs.

7. At the end of the session the children could give each special person a flower or a few chocolates wrapped in cellophane with a handmade card.

8. Encourage the children to take photographs of their special people with the digital cameras.

Ready for more?

▶ Fun and Games – Set 'low maintenance' games out on a few tables for grandparents to play with their grandchildren, e.g. picture dominoes, jigsaw puzzles, Jenga, Connect Four, Snap etc.

▶ Old-fashioned Games – encourage a discussion about what grandparents played when they were little.

▶ Sharing a story – have a selection of books available and somewhere comfortable for the grandparents to read a story to their grandchildren.

▶ Grandparents Musical Statues – In advance find out what music the grandparents liked when they were little and play the music for musical statues. This time ask the grandparents to dance with their grandchildren. If either grandparent or grandchild moves they both have to sit out. The winners are the last child and grandparent to be dancing.

▶ Slide Show – if you are lucky enough to have an Interactive Whiteboard or a large Digital Photograph Frame show children busy engaged in a selection of activities. This can be running in the background or everyone can stop and look at it together.

Links to the Early Learning Goals

KUW: 8
PSED: 1, 2, 4
CLL: 1, 2, 3, 4, 5

Celebrations and Festivals

St. George's Day
(23rd April)

Dragon Sock Puppet

What you need:

- a red sock (for each child)
- red craft foam or card
- scraps of red, yellow and orange craft foam
- red glitter glue/red sequins
- fabric glue
- wiggly eyes or black buttons
- a fabric pen
- aprons
- table covering

What you do:

1. Cut two wings and a tail from the red craft foam. Decorate with red glitter glue or red sequins.

2. Try the sock on the child's hand and decide where to put the eyes, wings and tail.

3. Lay the sock down flat and glue these parts on. Leave to dry thoroughly.

4. Whilst the glue is drying make the flames by cutting out three flame shapes of different sizes and colours from the craft foam. Glue them together – one on top of the other – large, middle, small.

5. Put the sock puppet on the child's hand and mark where the flames are to go – using their thumb as the bottom part of the dragon's mouth.

6. Remove the puppet and glue on the flames – make sure the pointed part of the flame (top) is coming 'out' of the mouth.

St. George's Day Flag

What you need:

I will need

▶ a piece of white material or white card (any size but no smaller than A4)

▶ small pieces of sponge or a paintbrush

▶ red poster paint

▶ aprons

▶ garden canes

▶ PVA glue or strong tape

▶ table covering

What you do:

1. Draw a cross with a pencil/fine pen on the card or material, or see if children can copy a cross themselves.

2. Explain to children that they have to print along the lines of the cross with the sponge, or paint the red line using the brush.

3. When dry, the flags can be fixed somewhere or attached to small garden canes using glue or strong tape.

St. George's Castle

What you need:

▶ a very large cardboard box (fridge/washing machine size)

▶ a sharp craft knife (only to be used by an adult)

▶ a St. George's flag on a stick/cane

What you do:

1. Open the box right out, trim off the bottom flaps so that the box stands up.

2. With a sharp knife cut out 'turret' shapes all around the top of the box.

3. Cut out a few slits for windows.

4. Finally, fly the St. George's flag from one of the turrets.

Sing a dragon song: Puff, The Magic Dragon

Puff the magic dragon
Lived by the sea
And frolicked in the Autumn mist
In a land called Honnah-Lee.

Little Jackie Paper
Loved that rascal, Puff,
And brought him strings and sealing wax
And other fancy stuff.

Chorus : Puff the magic dragon
   Lived by the sea
   And frolicked in the Autumn mist
   In a land called Honnah-Lee.

Together they would travel
On a boat with billowed sail
Jackie kept a lookout perched
On Puff's gigantic tail.

Noble kings and princes
Would bow whenever they came.
Pirate ships would lower their flags
When Puff called out their name.

Chorus : Puff the magic dragon
   Lived by the sea
   And frolicked in the Autumn mist
   In a land called Honnah-Lee.

Links to the Early Learning Goals

CLL: 3, 4, 5, 7

PD: 7, 8

PSED: 1, 2, 3, 4

KUW: 6, 8

CD: 1, 2, 3

Christmas

Santa's Workshop

What you need:

▶ a table or a big, sturdy box for the counter, decorated with tinsel

▶ an old telephone

▶ paper, order pads, a stamp pad and Christmas stamps, stapler, hole punch, selections of pens etc.

▶ a computer keyboard (for ordering more toys)

▶ a huge selection of boxes wrapped in cheap Christmas paper – all different sizes to encourage size language, sorting, counting etc

▶ a chute (a large plastic pipe or cardboard tube)

▶ a very big box to be used as Santa's sleigh – to be decorated by children with string, ribbons, bells, etc.

▶ Christmas dressing up clothes: santa, elf, fairy, reindeer, etc.

▶ a globe or world map

What you do:

1. Talk about where Santa lives – look at a globe or world map together. Look at how far he has to travel. Talk about how Santa knows how to get to children's houses. Talk about addresses. What do we look at to find our way?

2. Make a very simple 'picture map'. On your map put pictures (cut from old Christmas cards, gift wrap etc) of little trees, snowmen, snowy mountains. Put Santa's workshop at the start of a trail and then children's houses at the end. Draw a pathway from one side of the map to the other. Photocopy a larger version and put on the wall to prompt discussion.

3. Talk about what Santa has to do in order to deliver all the presents on time. On the table in Santa's workshop, put a large piece of card with 'Santa's List of Jobs' written at the top and provide a pen for children to write things down. Children can also have their own little 'To do' pads – encourage them to cross off the jobs as they do them!

4. Make a postbox and encourage letter writing to Santa by providing a selection of attractive paper that will appeal to the children. Collect used stamps to stick on them or use a rubber stamp. Don't forget to empty the postbox and take a real interest in the mail you collect. You could have a 'Christmas letter line'. This can be a rope, string or washing line attached to two posts or garden canes in buckets of sand. Make sure you ask the children to read their letters out loud or help them to. Santa can write back to the children – individually or a group letter. In the letters try to include something that is personal to the child/group.

5. Make signs for your Santa's workshop – 'Open', 'Closed', 'Back in 5 minutes' etc. Encourage the children to make their own signs and leave notes for Santa's elves. Have a calendar, a real clock etc. so children can be looking at and talking about the numbers on them.

6. Encourage 'telephone talk' in the workshop e.g., 'Hello! Santa's workshop – Can I help you?'

7. How many presents can they fit on the sleigh? Have a 'size sorting' chute (a plastic pipe or a large cardboard tube) to post different sized presents through.

8. You could also decorate the outdoor area of your setting with white sheets (cover pop up tents with white sheets for mountains). Stick up pictures of Christmas stockings, Santa, Rudolph etc. Have plenty of signs around e.g. 'North Pole – this way', 'Have you written to Santa?' etc. Put up some Christmas lights to add to the atmosphere.

Ready for more?

▶ Christmas Circle Time – Choose a festive tray to place about 5 Christmas objects on such as a tree decoration, Christmas cracker, small Christmas stocking, chocolate tree novelty, bell etc. Talk about the items on the tray and show them to the group. Ask the children if they know what they are? Explain the rules of the game – you will cover the tray with a cloth or a piece of material and remove an item from the tray (without them seeing). Ask a child to come out and take the cover off the tray. You can either ask that child to say which item is missing or ask the whole group. This is good for developing memory skills.

▶ Have a Christmas party – With traditional Christmas music, songs, games and food! See The Little Book of Christmas for more ideas!

▶ Email Santa – a safe and quick way to get a response www.email.santa.com/email_santa.asp

Links to the Early Learning Goals

CLL: 2, 3, 4, 5, 6, 7, 1, 19

PD: 1, 2, 8

PSED: 1, 2, 3, 7, 13

PSRN: 1, 2, 3, 9, 12

KUW: 1, 3, 6, 7, 8

CD: 1, 2, 3, 5

Wedding Day

A wedding topic is a big thing to cram into one day so maybe have a run up to the special day itself using the time to prepare invitations, artificial or paper flowers, food, gather outfits etc. Give yourselves plenty of time to collect dresses, outfits for the children to wear and to use for role-play.

What you need:

▶ photographs of weddings/a wedding photo album (those of children's parents, or weddings that they have attended)

▶ bride and groom outfits: see if anyone has been recently married and if you could borrow their dress/outfit to show the children. Maybe someone has their outfit in the loft and would share it for the day?

▶ bridesmaids' dresses: particularly those of small children, which may be used for the children to dress up in.

▶ a collection of bridal magazines for looking at/cutting up

▶ a camera to capture the day (or ask if a parent would come along and be 'photographer' for the session)

▶ music

▶ card and pens (to make wedding invitations)

▶ invitations/flowers/buffet food/confetti

▶ four-wheeled vehicle for wedding transport

What you do:

1. Look at wedding photographs and magazines and talk about what a wedding is.

2. Make wedding invitations.

3. Dress up in wedding clothes/fancy clothes.

4. Give opportunities for children to listen to different kinds of music. Decide what type would be suitable for a wedding and discuss why.

5. Set up part of your setting as the church area/registry office with a covered table and flowers and candlesticks. Conduct a mock ceremony to give some children an understanding of what exactly a wedding is. Two children volunteers will be the bride and groom, the rest of the children will be bridesmaids, groomsmen or guests. Make sure everyone has a turn to be part of the wedding party. One of the children or an adult could be the photographer.

6. What about presents? Children could make presents to give the 'couple'.

7. Bake a cake and decorate with white icing. Have after the 'ceremony'.

Ready for more?

▶ Talk about a wedding from another culture. Would the dress be different? The food? Look at the differences between religions and ceremonies. There may be children in your setting from different cultures who would be able to bring in photos, clothes and music. Or if you have any parents from culturally different backgrounds, use their experiences to widen your knowledge and that of the children.

Links to the Early Learning Goals

PSED: 1, 2, 4, 6, 11, 14   KUW; 2, 7, 9, 11

CLL: 1, 5, ,7 8, 17   PD: 1, 2, 7

PSRN: 1, 3 12   CD: 1, 2, 5

Easter

For Christians, Easter commemorates the resurrection of Christ after his crucifixion. Whilst attention needs to be paid to the religious context of Easter for most children it will have a totally different meaning! Chocolate eggs, Easter bonnets, Easter bunnies and egg hunts!

What you need:

- ▶ hard boiled eggs
- ▶ paints/felt pen/glue
- ▶ tea strainers
- ▶ ramps
- ▶ 'egg tokens'

- ▶ small bags
- ▶ cereal
- ▶ cooking chocolate
- ▶ mini eggs

What you do:

1. Make sure every child has a hard boiled egg. They can decorate it in any way they like. Provide materials to paint or draw on the eggs.

2. Have an egg race with each child using the egg that they have decorated! Depending on the number of children you have, split into two teams (or more) and have a relay type event (outdoors when possible) where the children race to a certain point with their egg in a tea strainer. When they reach the designated spot they then head back to their team, remove their egg and hand over the tea strainer to the next child in line. Encourage cheering for team mates!

3. Use the boiled eggs to have team ramp races. See whose egg gets down a ramp the quickest! The shells do tend to get smashed so do this activity after any others you have planned!

Ready for more?

▶ Easter Egg Hunt – prior to your 'Easter Day' print or draw lots of small eggs onto A4 paper. These can be one size or a variety sizes. Photocopy the page at least 10 times. Laminate and cut out to make 'egg tokens'. Hide indoors and outdoors. Provide everyone with a small bag or container to collect their egg tokens in. Have a small prize available for whoever finds the most tokens. Spend time counting the eggs together, discussing where they were found (on, under, behind etc) and cheering each time a total is announced!

▶ Make Simple Easter Bonnets – Using long pieces of card approx 2-3 inches wide, size these to children's heads and get them to decorate for quick, simple headdresses. Alternatively decorate paper plates or bowls (or a bowl glued to a plate). Attach two ribbons on the edges of the plate to tie under the chin. Or buy cheap straw hats from a pound shop and decorate these. Lots of little chicks/egg type decorations are available!

▶ Easter Nests – Melt chocolate in a bowl in a pan of boiling water, and then remove from pan and add a large bowl of your chosen cereal. Get the children to mix and then spoon into cake cases to make nests for mini eggs

Links to the Early Learning Goals

PSED: 1, 2, 3, 4, 6, 8, 14
CLL: 5, 7, 8, 17
PSRN: 1, 2, 3, 12

KUW: 1, 3, 7, 10, 11
PD: 1, 2, 5, 6, 7
CD: 1, 2, 5

Diwali

Diwali is a significant festival in Hinduism, Sikhism, Buddhism and Jainism and an official holiday in India. It signifies the renewal of life. It is often referred to as the 'Festival of Lights' because of the common practice of lighting small clay lamps (called diyas) and placing them all over the inside and outside of the home. The lights and other decorations are used to welcome visitors and hopefully the Goddess of Fortune – Lakshmi.

What you need:

- ▶ clay (air drying)
- ▶ tea lights
- ▶ paint
- ▶ PVA glue
- ▶ petals (fabric)
- ▶ flowers (cut out by the children from brightly coloured paper and card)
- ▶ coloured string
- ▶ thick straws, cut into sections of about 1.5cm
- ▶ coloured chalk/felt pens/pastels
- ▶ black paper
- ▶ strips of paper approximately 20cm wide (for the band/top of the door banner)
- ▶ shield-type shapes to attach to the long piece of the banner (optional)

What you do:

Clay lamps:

1. Encourage each child to use the clay to make a small bowl shape, the centre of which will need to be big enough to hold a tea light. For younger children, encourage them to roll the clay into a ball and then press a finger down into the middle. Pinch the clay with thumb and forefinger around the edge, gradually making a bowl shape.

2. Let the clay dry, then paint the outside, let that dry and then glue small colourful petals around the outside edge. Gently push petals into the wet clay, let that dry and then paint.

3. Finally place the tea light in the centre.

In certain parts of India it is customary to wear a necklace of fresh flowers (garland) at Diwali, and to hang an embroidered door hanging (or toran) above doorways.

Flower garlands:

Each child will need a length of string, with a knot at one end so that the flowers and straws cannot fall off!

Use petals from artificial flowers/or boxes of petals that can be bought from many outlets.

1. Encourage threading, one flower and then one piece of straw, or several flowers of different colours and then straws to separate every so often.

2. When complete tie a knot to make sure all flowers stay on the string.

Door hanging:

1. Use long lengths of paper for the band which is the top of the banner.

2. Lay the paper on the floor and offer children a choice of resources to make a pattern along its length. If children are able, offer them the chance to cut out shield-shaped pieces of paper. Once these too are decorated they can then be stuck to the bottom of the bands already decorated.

3. Hang around your setting!

Rangoli:

Hindus draw a colourful design called a Rangoli on the floor near the entrance to their home. The Rangoli patterns are traditionally drawn with the fingers using flour, rice grains or coloured chalk and can be square, circular, rectangular, or a mix of all three. They are often symmetrical and the design taken from nature

1. First, show children Rangoli patterns for inspiration and then encourage them to try for themselves on black paper. The grid is usually made from small dots at regular intervals over a specific shape and then these dots can be joined together to create a design.

2. Work outside on the playground or on paving slabs. Use white chalk to get an outline of the design and the coloured chalks to fill it in. Use a mixture of flour, water and food colouring to make a paste and create your Rangoli. (Note: It will be semi-permanent and might possibly not ever be fully removed so be careful where you work!)

Ready for more?

▶ Food is very important during Diwali so why not offer the children Indian sweets and snacks to taste? Where possible, get advice from someone who is familiar with Diwali celebration food.

▶ Offer opportunities for the children to hear Indian music.

▶ Let the children dress up in costumes/materials that are of vibrant colours and lend themselves to light and illumination themes.

▶ Supply books to encourage the children to look at India and its customs more closely, and to look at Rangoli patterns.

▶ Diwali is incomplete without fireworks so why not do outdoor splash painting or use the whiteboard to create firework pictures.

Links to the Early Learning Goals

PSED: 1, 2, 3, 4, 5, 6 8, 12

CLL: 1, 3, 5, 7 8, 17

PSRN: 1, 11, 12

KUW: 1, 2, 3, 4, 8 10, 11

PD: 1, 2, 7, 8

CD: 1, 2, 3, 4, 5

Chinese New Year

Chinese New Year is a time of feasting, celebration, fireworks and gift giving. Try making some of these colourful decorations to display in your setting.

What you need:

- ▶ scissors
- ▶ glue/sellotape/stapler
- ▶ brightly coloured stiff paper or card approx A4 size
- ▶ stickers/pens/paint
- ▶ clay (air drying)/plasticine
- ▶ brown or green pipe cleaners (thick ones if possible)
- ▶ pink tissue paper
- ▶ PVA glue
- ▶ black paper
- ▶ glitter
- ▶ egg cartons (cardboard)

What you do:

Chinese lanterns:

1. Encourage the children to decorate one side of a piece of stiff paper or card with paint, felt pens, stickers, etc.

2. Fold the paper lengthways down the middle with the decoration on the outside. From one end cut a strip approx 2cm wide and put to the side for use later (this will be the handle).

3. Cut slits from the fold almost to the outside edge – again leaving about 2cm not cut. Do this all along the paper. You will have approximately 9 cuts. Then unfold the paper, put glue along one of the shorter edges (top or bottom of the paper) and stick to the opposite edge. You will now have a lantern shape.

4. Using tape or glue fix the handle to the top edge of your lantern in two places. Hang to display.

Plum blossom tree:

1. Twist together 2 different lengths of pipe cleaner but as you move up the length, the pipe cleaners need to part company and look like branches of a tree. Repeat this approximately 5-6 times to create all of your branches.

2. Lay the branches on the table and at various points dot on a little PVA glue. Leave about 3cm at the end without glue as this will be stuck into a base of clay or plasticine which will be the bottom of the tree.

3. Cut or tear the tissue paper into small pieces and then scrunch it up, and push it down onto the glue. Leave to dry.

4. When dry, make holes in the clay or plasticine base for your branches to stick into (using a clay tool or thin pencil). Press the pipe cleaners/branches into the holes.

Chinese fireworks:

1. Look at pictures or photographs of fireworks for inspiration!

2. Using small squeezable bottles, cotton buds or thin paintbrushes let the children apply glue onto a piece of paper to create a pattern.

3. Then, wherever they have applied glue the children shake some glitter. Tap off the excess and then you have your creation left behind. For a 3D look use silicone filler instead of glue.

4. Display on the wall.

Ready for more?

▶ **Chinese dragon:**

1. Cut up an egg box. Paint each egg 'cup' on the outside – use as many as you want. The more you use the longer the dragon.

2. When dry, paint the inside of one egg cup black – this will be the dragon's head and the inside of his mouth. Thread string through the top of the dragon's mouth, so it will fit sideways against the other egg cups, and then thread through each of the sides of the egg cups to string them all together. Knot either end of the string.

3. Inside the black egg cup attach a little bit of red paper for a tongue and stick two paper eyes on the top edge of the cup.

Links to the Early Learning Goals

PSED: 1, 2, 3, 5, 6, 7, 8, 12, 13, 14   **KUW:** 1, 2, 4, 5, 6, 11

CLL: 1, 2, 3, 5, 7, 8, 17   **PD:** 1, 7, 8

PSRN: 10, 12   **CD:** 1, 2, 3, 5

Valentine's Day

Why not make Valentine's Day a 'special friends day' in your setting? Let the children make cards, heart-shaped snacks and decorations and take the time to let each other know that they are good friends and to share the things they like about each other.

I will need

What you need:

- ▶ coloured paper and white card
- ▶ glue and scissors
- ▶ heart-shaped stickers
- ▶ heart-shaped sponge (for printing)
- ▶ small jars
- ▶ plain cotton material
- ▶ fabric pens/paint
- ▶ elastic bands/ribbon
- ▶ bread
- ▶ condensed milk
- ▶ a new paintbrush
- ▶ heart-shaped dough/biscuit cutters

What you do:

Heart caterpillar:

1. Depending on the age of your children, you may need to prepare lots of cut out hearts in advance for this activity. Alternatively you could supply a heart-shaped template for the child to draw around and then cut out. Use one or more colours for the hearts.

2. Once cut out, start sticking the hearts slightly on top of each other as though you are stacking them. Make your heart caterpillar as long or as short as you want.

3. Finally add the last heart, the opposite way up, this will be the caterpillar's head. Draw a face on this heart. You may also want to add antennae which have tiny little hearts on the end. Use very thin strips of paper or pipe cleaners.

Valentine candy jars:

1. Prior to this special day send out a 'wanted' note to parents to see if you can collect enough small baby food jars or similar sized containers so that each child has one to decorate.

2. Let each child decorate a jar with stickers, etc. Also get each child to decorate on a circular piece of plain cotton material which is going to cover the top of the jar.

3. Fill each jar with tiny sweets. Use the cotton circles to cover the jars and attach with an elastic band or ribbon.

4. At the end of your special Valentine's day, each child gives another child a jar. The point is to make sure everyone takes a gift home.

Valentine snacks:

1. Mix together approximately 10ml of condensed milk and gradually add red food colouring. Add as much colouring as you wish until you have the shade of red you want.

2. Then using a new paintbrush paint a heart on a piece of bread and toast it!

3. Alternatively, use a heart shaped dough/biscuit cutter to cut out scone or biscuit mixture.

4. Have all your food at snack time heart-shaped or red!

Ready for more?

▶ Turn heart caterpillars into butterflies: make four more rows of stacked hearts and attach them to the body of the heart caterpillar at an angle (two on each side of its body) and you have a butterfly! Alternatively you could just add two large hearts (one on each side) to the caterpillar body.

▶ Don't forget the Valentine's cards! Each child designs one of their own and posts it in your setting's postbox. At the end of the session hand them out – one to each child, but not the one they made. Talk about friendship and caring.

▶ Have a Valentine's dance! Let the children use red ribbons and scarves to make up a dance for their friends!

Links to the Early Learning Goals

PSED: 1, 2 3, 4, 5, 7, 8, 12

CLL: 1, 2, 3, 4, 7, 8, 17

PSRN: 10, 11, 12

KUW: 1, 6, 7

PD: 1, 2, 7, 8

CD: 1, 2, 3, 5

Pancake Day

Why not make pancakes with the children in your setting and indulge away!

What you need:

▶ 100g of flour
▶ 2 eggs
▶ 300ml semi skimmed milk
▶ a pinch of salt
▶ 1 tablespoon of sunflower oil
▶ a frying pan
▶ plates
▶ fruit and yoghurt

What you do:

1. Put the flour and a pinch of salt into a large mixing bowl, and make a well in the middle. Crack two eggs into this well, and then add the oil and about 50ml of milk.

2. Gradually whisk the fluid in the centre of the bowl into the flour, incorporating the flour gradually. Continue until the mixture has a smooth, thick paste-like consistency. Add a little more milk if your mixture is too thick.

3. Then steadily add the remainder of the milk, whisking constantly so that gradually the batter becomes the consistency of thick cream.

4. Heat the pan over a medium heat and wipe it around with oiled kitchen paper.

5. Carefully spoon or pour some mixture into the pan, to cover the bottom evenly. You may need to tilt the pan a little to get even coverage.

6. Cook for about half a minute, gently moving the pan from side to side to encourage it not to stick. Then flip to turn the pancake over! The flip can also be achieved using a spatula.

7. Cook for a few more seconds and then tilt the pan so the pancake slides out onto the plate.

8. Once you have the pancake cooked what will you serve it with? Why not try fresh fruits and low fat yoghurts?

Ready for more?

▶ You may be in a setting with little or no access to a cooker or kitchen. Nowadays you can buy pre-cooked pancakes that only need to be warmed in a microwave. If your setting doesn't usually house a microwave see if you can borrow one for the session.
Your emphasis then could be on the preparation of the fillings. Encourage children to fill and roll or fold their own pancake.

▶ Whilst some children may manage to 'flip' their pancake, many children will not be able to do so. Why not use frying pans from the home corner and cut out cardboard pancakes for them to flip instead?

and more?

▶ Have pancake races using pretend pancakes and a pan – running between two specified spots!

▶ Look to see if you have any books about pancakes or can think of any stories that could be altered to include a pancake? Book suggestions: 'The Big Pancake' (Baxter & Kenyon), 'Pancakes, Pancakes' (Eric Carle), 'Mr. Wolf's Pancakes' (Jan Fearnley) and 'Mama Panya's Pancakes' (Mary and Rich Chaimberlain).

Links to the Early Learning Goals

PSED: 1, 2, 3, 4, 8

CLL: 1, 2, 3, 4, 5, 7, 8

PSRN: 1, 2, 3, 9, 11, 12

KUW: 1, 3, 4, 7

PD: 1, 2, 4, 5, 7

CD: 1, 2, 5

The **Little Books** series consists of:

All Through the Year
Bags, Boxes & Trays
Bricks and Boxes
Celebrations
Christmas
Circle Time
Clay and Malleable Materials
Clothes and Fabrics
Colour, Shape and Number
Cooking from Stories
Cooking Together
Counting
Dance
Dance, with music CD
Discovery Bottles
Dough
50
Fine Motor Skills
Fun on a Shoestring
Games with Sounds
Growing Things
ICT
Investigations
Junk Music
Language Fun
Light and Shadow

Listening
Living Things
Look and Listen
Making Books and Cards
Making Poetry
Mark Making
Maths Activities
Maths from Stories
Maths Songs and Games
Messy Play
Music
Nursery Rhymes
Outdoor Play
Outside in All Weathers
Parachute Play
Persona Dolls
Phonics
Playground Games
Prop Boxes for Role Play
Props for Writing
Puppet Making
Puppets in Stories
Resistant Materials
Role Play
Sand and Water
Science through Art
Scissor Skills

Sewing and Weaving
Small World Play
Special Days
Stories from around the World
Sound Ideas
Storyboards
Storytelling
Seasons
Time and Money
Time and Place
Treasure Baskets
Treasureboxes
Tuff Spot Activities
Washing Lines
Writing

All available from

www.acblack.com/featherstone